POOR MAN'S GAME

PICKUP ARTIST TECHNIQUES FROM A GUY WHO WORKS AT A GAS STATION

RIFF HOLSER

SOY SAUCE PUBLISHING

Legal Notice

This book is for adults only.

This book provides general advice for educational and entertainment purposes only. Copying, distributing, or transmitting any part of this book is strictly prohibited. The reader is responsible for being aware of and obeying all applicable laws in their area or jurisdiction. The author and publisher assume no responsibility and disclaim any liability for anything the reader chooses to do. The advice presented is not a substitute for professional or legal advice, and readers should consult with a licensed professional if needed. The author and publisher disclaim liability for errors or omissions and any actions taken based on the information provided. Trademarks mentioned are for descriptive purposes only and do not imply endorsement. There is no intention to cause offense to any particular individuals or entities, and any such offense is unintentional.

CONTENTS

INTRODUCTION

Hi, you don't know me, or maybe you do. The name's Riff. Perhaps our paths have crossed or perhaps not. If you've ever met me, I'm a guy who works at a gas station. No, it's not the greatest job in the world, it's nothing compared to being a programmer or a doctor, but I do get women. And I know a ton of secrets about what works with women and what doesn't. You'd be surprised at all the things I know that you probably never guessed a guy who works at a gas station would know. But out of all the things I know, my knowledge in regards to how to get jiggy with the opposite sex is far in excess of what the common man knows, and some have even told me I'm a genius.

I've worked at my local gas station for 30 years, pumping gas and washing off windshields. Yeah, you don't see many workers doing that nowadays, but in my small town that's still a thing.

And before I go further, you might be doubtful, you might be thinking to yourself, 'Why in the fubble does this guy working at a gas station for 30 years know anything about meeting women? Don't you have to be rich to meet any kind of decent woman these days?'

Ha ha, I get you! Most people wonder that. But truth be told, it's because I work at a gas station that I have nothing else to focus on outside of work except for meeting women. I mean, I can't afford the fancy VR headset or the streaming movie subscription that you might have, and I always thought I was a good singer, but I can't afford a microphone. But meeting women, that's free, it doesn't cost me a dime to meet women. And over the years I must have been on something like 10,000 dates.

Now I know you might be thinking to yourself, 'This guy can't be serious, it costs a lot of money to take a woman on a date, and 10,000 dates, that must have cost a fortune.'

Well looky here, bub, let me explain it to you. That is why you picked up this book, isn't it? So that someone could explain it to you.

Yes, yes, I get it, you're thinking that guys should spend lots and lots of money on women, and it's probably not in your reality that a guy with no dough can get women, let alone be able to take a woman out on a date.

I often hear bad dating advice that men give other men, which goes something like this, "If you don't have money, you won't get any women, you need to make a lot of money first, and then you get the women."

And maybe that dating advice has some truth to it, but I sure as heck wouldn't know, because I've never had enough money to be able to test that theory. But I can say with 100% certainty that you don't need any money to get women. I mean, you can't be a beggar, begging a woman to buy things for you. You need to at least be self-sustainable, but you don't need to pay a dime to be able to meet women or take them out on dates. And in this book, I'm going to explain how I do it. How I meet women, how I take them out on dates, and how I always have women calling me wanting to see me, even though I'm always broke and work at a gas station.

That said, you don't need to be poor to make this stuff work, you just need to be you.

Now before we delve into it, I'd like to, first of all, thank you for buying this book, and after my publisher takes his cut, I plan to put whatever royalty I get from your purchase into a retirement fund, something I just started, so that when I'm too old to pump gas I won't become homeless. Thus, I'm truly thankful for your interest in the advice I have to give, advice which many have told me was the most amazing advice they've ever been told about getting women. In fact, the whole reason I wrote this book is because guys whose dating lives I'd saved urged me to write it.

CHAPTER 1
GET YOUR MIND IN ORDER

SO BEFORE WE start getting you to the point where you can even start to meet women, we need to, first of all, get your mind in order.

And to get your mind in order, the first thing we need to do is kill any insecurities you might have.

You see, the reason most men truly fail with women is because they have insecurities, their mind always starts to think about their negative points or things that others will judge.

So to kill our insecurities, we need to enter something I call Peak State.

If you're thinking to yourself, 'What is peak state?' and 'How can I enter it?' then good, because it means your mind is in the right place to move forward. If you were thinking something totally different, no worries, we're going to move forward anyway.

So peak state is basically a state of mind where you feel truly happy, alert, not focused on your insecurities at all, and totally in the zone.

How to get into peak state is going to be different for

everyone, but you can actually get yourself into peak state at will.

So the next question you should be thinking is, 'How can I get into peak state at will?'

What I want you to do is to imagine a time in your life where you were most in the zone, it could have been playing a video game where everything was working perfectly for you and you had gotten a new high score or reached a new level, or it could have been that time you kept getting the basketball in the hoop or whatever it was. Some of you might need to close your eyes to properly imagine things, and that's okay. I want you to imagine you're there at that time, and everything is going absolutely perfect for you, you are in the zone man! Feel that feeling of being totally in the zone! Yes, that's the feeling! I want you to feel that feeling for all it's worth, and now look around with eyes open. Boom! You're in peak state now! You're back in the zone!

If you did things right, you should feel a smile creeping up on your face, all of your past traumas or whatever should melt away, and you feel just completely present and totally awesome!

For some of you, you might need to try a few times to get there, but the more you attempt this exercise, the faster and more easily you'll get there. Basically, your subconscious mind will start to understand what you're trying the more you try, and you'll more quickly and more effortlessly get there every time. It's essentially a way of tricking your mind to replicate a past time when you were in the zone.

If you're just reading or listening to this book and not actually trying what I'm telling you to do. I want you to put the book down, or if you're listening to it I want you to pause, and I want you to actually try to do what I just told you to do, and clearly visualize a past time when you were in the zone. Because you really need to know how to do this, and not just once, you need to get into a regular habit of doing this so your subconscious mind knows what you're trying to do every time you do this and puts you in peak state every time.

If you've got the technique down, then great. If not, then keep practicing it until you get there. If you feel like you've never been in the zone before in your whole life, then choose the closest memory you have when you were in a state close to being in the zone, or another way would be to choose a time in your life when you were in your happiest state.

If you have trouble doing this exercise and can't seem to get into peak state at all, that's fine, not everyone can, and it's not the end of the world, but it will help a lot if you do have the ability to get into peak state at will, so I urge you to keep trying. But if you truly cannot achieve peak state, then in future chapters when I talk about achieving peak state, I simply want you to remember your happiest memory and at the very least it should make you feel happy to remember a happy memory, and that should suffice.

CHAPTER 2
MONEY

SO THE THING that differentiates Poor Man's Game from other forms of game is that you will be doing game without spending any of your own money except on things that you normally spend money on. This includes paying your half for your meals when eating with a woman, whether eating at home or going out to eat, paying your half for taxis or ride shares if you and a woman both agree that you need to pay for one, and pretty much paying your half of any expenses that would be incurred in any kind of activities that you do together with a woman.

However, if a woman becomes your girlfriend, then there are certain days of the year where you have to give them a gift, like their birthday or during the holidays, and so if you have a girlfriend, then buying them gifts is not something that is optional, you must bear that expense, though they should also be buying you gifts at those times of year as well.

All of that said, if a woman should offer to pay for anything, it's up to you whether you want to insist that you pay your half or that you accept their offer to pay. In my case, I always accept when a woman offers to pay for anything, since I am indeed a poor man, and so anything I have to pay for would be a big hit to my pocket.

As you meet more and more women, some will be at the same income level as you and that's fine, and some will make a lot more than you, while others will make much less than you. However, you should not assess a woman based on her financial status, you should only assess a woman based on if they are compatible with you or not. And this should work both ways, as a woman should not assess you based on your financial status.

Any woman who tries to judge you based on your income is simply not a woman for you, and not the kind of woman you want to be with no matter what your financial status, because it's not all about the money. Furthermore, you've chosen your career, whether you work at a gas station like me, do some similar low-paying job, or perhaps you make much more than me but are financially savvy and have created a budget for yourself that doesn't include spending money frivolously.

Some might think that women will only go for rich guys. However, a lot of the wealthiest rich men are penny-pinchers, because that's what enabled them to get to achieve great wealth. For example, if we look at Warren Buffet, the billion-aire investor, he actually counts the pennies spent when he buys his meal at McDonald's every morning. So being thrifty is not something to be looked down upon, but rather smart money management, and any intelligent person with a halfway decent understanding of finances and budgeting will understand that, and should respect the fact that you have a budget and that you manage your money well as a self-sustainable man.

So as a financially savvy poor man, and you've got to be financially savvy if you're poor, when you're meeting different women, you're not going to do anything differently than you normally do with your money. And so, it may make more financial sense, as well as be healthier, to eat a cheap meal at home with a woman as opposed to eating a fancy meal out at some extravagant restaurant. And you've really got to hold true to your principles on this, meaning that you should never feel that you have to spend more than what your budget would normally entail in order to impress a woman. And you need to make this clear to any woman early on, that you are financially savvy and that you have a budget because you believe in being smart with your money, and you don't believe in throwing money away on meaningless things.

It's possible that you might meet some women who have different ideas of what saving and spending may mean, and that's fine as long as they are open-minded enough to understand that although you may be thrifty, you are financially savvy, and perhaps they could even learn a thing or two from you about managing their finances. Because if a woman normally throws away five dollars on a coffee at a cafe when she could be making a similar coffee at home for 20 cents, she's throwing away four dollars and 80 cents that could be better put in an index fund earning something like 10% in interest every year, or at least in a savings account earning some kind of interest rate. While it's true that when we pay for a coffee at a cafe, we're paying for the environment, is that four-dollar and 80-cent environment really so much better than the public library or your local park? Because throwing away four dollars and 80 cents for environment is losing so much more than just four dollars and 80 cents, because you're also losing all that compound interest that you'd have if you simply put that four dollars and 80 cents in an index fund or savings account.

You see, just because you're a poor man doesn't mean you're really poor, it means you are financially savvy. And if you're actually a guy who isn't very financially savvy, you're still savvy enough to realize that you'll get interest on your money putting it in certain kinds of accounts, and that making coffee at home is cheaper than buying coffee at a cafe.

Being poor though, you kind of have to be financially savvy in order to survive, even though you might not be well-versed in all the financial jargon, and that's fine.

Point is, if a woman can't understand the advantage of saving money, that's fine, as long as she respects you and your penny-pinching mentality. And you should never feel a need to have to use money in order to impress a woman, which means you have to be okay to lose some women who simply cannot accept you for who you are and for your ways of thinking about money.

CHAPTER 3
BOSS BEHAVIOR

AS RIDICULOUS AS THIS SOUNDS, I want you to imagine yourself as a character who is a boss. As in, not a boss that takes orders from another boss, but a top guy who spends his whole day dishing out commands to those below him, and never takes orders from anyone.

How does a boss think? He thinks the world is there to serve him, and his demeanor gives off this vibe.

How does a boss stand? He stands straight and very still, back completely erect, unwavering.

Is a boss calm? Yes, he's always calm and relaxed, since he's comfortable in his own skin and has no worries.

How does a boss move? Being someone with no worries and generally always calm and relaxed, he generally moves at his own leisurely pace.

Does a boss get all butt-hurt when something doesn't go his way? Not really, the thought of something not going his way is completely outside of his reality, so he's mostly entertained by it rather than feeling all butt-hurt.

Does a boss react to being rejected? No, not really, a boss rejects others, but when someone rejects him it tends to be so far out of his reality that he just laughs.

Does a boss fear losing a woman that he's talking to? No, not really, a boss has no fear. If a woman walks away from him, little goes through his mind other than perhaps, 'She must be having a bad day.'

How does a boss sit in a chair? He always leans back, and moves very little.

How does a boss talk? He's got a sense of humor that's directly tied to his need for self-amusement, but other than that he's generally a man of few words whose comments are often short and to the point.

The key takeaways of this chapter, if you took nothing else from it, are:

1. Move slowly in social settings, as a boss would.

2. Be completely non-reactive, unfazed, or simply laugh, at any rejections, insults, or slights.

3. Stand completely erect. And when sitting, lean back.

4. Be a man of few words, unless you've decided to make a joke for the purpose of amusing yourself.

CHAPTER 4
WHERE AND HOW TO MEET WOMEN

WHERE YOU CAN MEET women mostly depends on where you live, but basically, I want you to go to places where lots of women might be. This could be a busy street, your local mall, a park, a bar, etc. It can literally be anywhere.

And I want you to find a nice spot to stand, like a boss would, a place where you have a good view of most of the people around, and where you're out of the way of being trampled on by a crowd. And I want you to think about that time when you were in the zone, and put yourself in peak state. And then what you do is you look around for women that look attractive to you.

Now when you see an attractive woman, what do you do? Well, you just walk right up to her, like a boss would. And you immediately start talking to her. And this is where a lot of guys freak-out, because they are too afraid to approach a woman they don't know and they have no clue what they're going to say to her.

The fear of approaching a woman never really goes away, but it does help if you have something in your mind to say to her upon making your approach. What tends to work best in almost all cases is to pick an article of clothing she's wearing and compliment that. How you structure your compliment is just as important, like if you just say, "Those are cool jeans," that will work, but if you say something more like, "I like how the aqua blue color of your jeans matches with your aqua blue lipstick," it'll likely land more effectively. Basically, any compliment on her clothing means you're complimenting her fashion sense, and if you compliment how two articles of her clothing go together, you're complimenting her ability to choose two items that look good together.

Now to take things a step further, you can say something like, "You must be a fashion designer. Oh, wow, I actually need help with getting my fashion together, maybe you can give me some pointers." A line like that can be used as a reason for her to meet up with you on a date where she can teach you the things she knows about fashion.

However, you don't have to get that advanced. Just a, "Wow! Cool jeans," will do.

And actually, you want to say this first line to every single woman you meet, this is your opening line. But if the next woman you meet isn't wearing jeans, of course you need to alter your opener to something similar like "Wow! Cool skirt!." And you also want to adjust your first line now and then to experiment, to see if something else might work better for you.

The whole point of having an opening line is so that when you approach a woman, you don't have to think about what you're going to say, since what you're going to say you will have said to many women before. And the more times you say it the more routine it will feel for you. And since what you're saying is going to be routine, this will allow you to focus more on you overcoming your fear of talking to a woman you don't know, as well as being able to say it a bit better every time with better vocal tonality. The more we say something, the better we get at saying it is basically how it goes. For example, if you give a speech just one time, it might go over okay, but if you were to give that same speech a hundred times, by the hundredth time you don't even have to consciously think about it.

After you say your opening line, she's going to then react either positively to it, or negatively to it. So then we have to choose what to say next if she reacts positively, and choose what to say if she reacts negatively. And after approaching many more women, how you respond to each positive or negative response will become routine as well.

This process of turning conversations with women who you don't know into routines through practice is an integral part of Poor Man's Game, and this is the system that is ultimately going to help you get dates with the types of women you like.

Sometimes, you'll approach a woman and say your opening line, and then she'll either react positively or negatively, and then you'll say something else based on her reaction, and then she'll throw something out of left field that leaves you without words. That's good, because it'll make your game better, since you can think about it after the interaction, and then the next time a woman you approach says the same thing, you'll know exactly what to say.

And so our process of how to meet women will be to walk up to a woman, say our opening line, see how she reacts, then say something else, and if she says something like, "I have a boyfriend," then we move on, back to our spot, and look around for the next woman to approach, who we then approach with the same or near-same opening line. And we just repeat this process again and again and again, until we click with a woman.

For guys new to everything I just said, it might take 400 approaches to be able to find a woman you click with, or it could take more, or it could take less, but it will eventually happen for you.

However, the good news is that the better you get at this,

the less approaches it will take each time to find the next woman who clicks with you. For me, since I've done this a lot, I'm able to click with about one in every 10 women I approach. And sometimes I get lucky, and things go well off my first approach. It all varies pretty greatly. But it wasn't always like that for me, when I first started this stuff, it did take me approximately 400 approaches in order to find a woman who clicked with me. And so as you see, I have improved quite a bit from when I first started. However, unlike you, I didn't have a book like this one to give me pointers. Though even with this book, be prepared for a little rejection, but don't let the rejections get you down, because to get good at game you just have to take your lumps like everyone else, and if you have the courage to keep going in spite of all the rejections, you will get better. It's the same as learning any sport, because at first you will no doubt suck, and the more you practice the better you get, and meeting women is very much like that, like getting good at a sport, it's not simply mentally knowing what to do, but as you practice your body physically learns what to do as well.

So, now that we've come to the end of this chapter, to start on this journey, you're going to have to meet at least 1 to 3 new women a day, every day, and by 'Meet' I mean approach. Can you do that? I hope you can, because that's what you're going to need to do. That's 365 to 1,095 women a year. And if you can do that for at least one year and a half, you should have built up your own little network of women that click with you, or at the very least met at least one woman who clicked with you, but either or isn't bad if you've got nothing on your plate.

Also, you can't look at this journey of meeting women every day as some kind of impossible task that you don't want to do, you have to want to do this, you have to force yourself to enjoy the process, the process of approaching and trying to talk to women. If you can enjoy the process, and at least do the bare minimum of one approach a day, then you'll soon be a very happy camper. Approaching women is non-optional, because that's what separates those who get good at game from those who have no game, in that those who get good at game force themselves to do approaches, regardless of how scared they are.

Of course, not approaching women is easy, you can just watch women walk by and do nothing, but doing nothing is not going to get you anywhere. You need to be walking up to women and starting conversations. You need to be walking up to women and finding out about them. If you finish this book, and you don't approach women, then you're going to be in a lot more pain, because you'll know what could be possible if you just put in the effort.

Yes, it's not easy! Yes, it takes courage! Yes, you're going to have to battle all these voices in your head telling you to not approach that attractive woman that just walked by you, that you know you'd love to approach if you could just drum up the courage to do so.

It's actually sad to me that so many guys give up before they ever do their first approach, and then complain about how game doesn't work. Well if it truly doesn't work, then how do you know that if you don't test the theory and simply approach one woman a day for a year and a half or so? Have you ever been lost and asked a stranger for directions? Well, it's not actually so different than that. So why is it that you could ask a woman for directions, but you can't muster up the courage to simply compliment a woman on an item of clothes that she's wearing? And I know you know the answer, and that answer is 'Fear.'

You will have to get over your fear. And the best way to do that is putting yourself into peak state, and knowing what your opening line will be, and just walking up to that attractive woman that you don't know and saying your opening line. Yes, you might get rejected, but that's all part of the learning process. The first time you tried to shoot a basketball in the hoop it probably didn't go in either. That's why you can't just approach one woman and then give up forever if things don't go as well as you'd initially planned. You're going to need to take many shots before that ball finally goes through the hoop.

So even if you have intense fear, that's okay, but just try to do just one approach anyway, in spite of your fear. I know if you put your mind to it, you can do it. And if you keep at it, you can be a superstar at this, and it all starts with that first approach.

CHAPTER 5
BODY LANGUAGE

IN ALL OF YOUR APPROACHES, aside from knowing what to say, I can't stress the importance of body language, and so it deserves its own chapter in this book in order to reiterate the point. And when I say the importance of body language, I mean you need to be consciously aware of how you walk and where your posture is at, at least at first.

You need to walk, stand, and talk like a boss. This means you need to stand erect, no slouching, chin up, shoulders back, etc. And you need to walk like you stand, completely erect, chin up, shoulders back. And try to hold eye contact when you're talking to a woman, if she's not looking at you, then fine. But if she is looking at you, you'd better be looking into her eyes as you talk to her.

So many guys are completely unaware of what their body is doing and think it doesn't make a difference in how they come across to women. But let me tell you, your body language is as important if not more important than the words coming out of your mouth, because women subconsciously pick up on it, and bad body language means low self-confidence, and there is nothing more unattractive to most women than guys who lack self-confidence.

Any book worth its weight about being successful with the opposite sex is going to cover body language, and Poor Man's Game is no different. So many times I've had guys tell me that they're approaching women and that they're saying the right things but they're just not getting any success, and I always say, "Show me your game, go approach that woman right there right now." And usually what they're doing wrong isn't what they say or do, but that once they start talking they have lost track of their body language, and either their head bobs up and down, or they naturally slouch forward, moving their head in to talk to a woman. A boss would not move their head forward to talk to a woman, a boss would stand firm and erect, and the woman should be moving their head forward because they're so interested in what this man with boss-like body language has to say.

This is how attraction is built, and it's very basic Pickup 101 type stuff. It's nothing new or revolutionary that I'm telling you here. But it does beg the question, 'Why is body language so darn important?' And my answer to you is do you even realize how hard it is for a man to get laid these days? All odds are working against you, nothing is in your favor. So any little things you can do to put the odds in your favor will greatly help you succeed with a woman. Having good body language can make the difference from being rejected to having your wildest fantasies come true, so damn right you want to make sure your body language is on point.

If you're coming from a position where you've never cared about body language before, and always slouched forward all your life or had other such bad habits, then you need to make a greater effort to consciously be aware of what body language you're projecting, and you need to correct it until it becomes natural for you to maintain an erect posture, keep your chin up, etc. Because, as you now should know, having good body language will have a significant impact on how successful you are with women when you approach and start a conversation with them. And it's a point most guys have problems with and are not aware of, but now you are aware of it.

CHAPTER 6
THE FIRST 20 TO 40 MINUTES

SO WE'VE COVERED GETTING the conversation started, but it's a far cry from what we need to know to fully understand what we need to do to be able to talk to women. That said, being able to start a conversation with a woman is what most guys see as being the hardest part. However, once you've got that down, you're on the right path to meeting many women.

We're going to assume from this point that you've figured out where and how to meet women, and that you've also got your body language in check. But beyond that, there's a lot more to cracking the puzzle. You see, it's entirely probable that one could approach and meet women and fail over and over again, never getting a number, and having nothing to show for their efforts; and we don't want that to happen. So in this chapter, we're going to cover exactly what you need to be doing to get beyond the mere formalities of getting to a point where you've been able to start a conversation with a woman. We need to get you to the point where your conversations with women actually build attraction. And in order to do that, we need to discuss the flow of conversation and how it should go.

So essentially, the conversation between most guys who have the courage to approach a woman will go something like this:

"That's a cool shirt. My name's John, what's your name? What are your hobbies? What kind of music do you like? What are you doing in this area?" etc, etc.

Now the problem here is two-fold. The first issue is that millions of other guys out of all the guys with the courage to actually approach and talk to a woman are doing that same thing. These are basically all interview-style questions where you ask questions and the woman answers your questions. And what you'll find is that by conducting your conversations in an interview-style manner, your conversations will quickly die, as in burn to the ground, the woman will lose attraction for you, and you'll soon find yourself walking away thinking to yourself, 'What did I do wrong?'

So I'll tell you what you did wrong, and that is that you asked a bunch of questions, which then forces the woman to think in order to produce answers. Furthermore, the woman probably has had many other guys walk up to her and ask these same questions, and nothing ever went anywhere from that, so the moment you start asking the same questions that many other guys in the past who failed with her have asked, she quickly starts to see you as just another one of those guys not worth her time, and she'll usually reject you pretty quickly as a result. I say 'Usually,' because if she's going through a rough time in her life, she might welcome a conversation with another human and you may get somewhere with that approach. Also, if you've been doing this stuff for a while, and you're game is really tight, then it will be possible to get an interview-style conversation to work. But in general, for most guys, an interview-style conversation off an approach will most likely lead to your demise if you attempt it.

Rather what you need to be doing is something that the

majority of other guys are not doing. So instead of asking questions, I'm going to suggest that you make statements, and give her opportunities to respond to those statements. It is indeed okay to ask questions if you need to, but you want 90 to 100% of your conversation with the woman to be you making statements, and then her saying whatever she's going to say, at least in the beginning before you get to know her better. The whole purpose of this is you remove the interview style dynamic, and remove any pressure that will cause her to think and feel like she has to answer. In case you didn't know, women hate being pressured.

So your conversation is better to go like this: "That's a cool shirt - PAUSE - My name's John - PAUSE - You look like someone who's into meditation - PAUSE - I know you like meditation because you have meditative eyes - PAUSE - I really love rock music, you seem like you're into rock music too - PAUSE - I'm not sure why I think you're into rock, I just get that sense from you - PAUSE - You're here today because you were expecting to meet a new guy - PAUSE."

Everywhere I said, 'PAUSE,' is giving her space to say something or ask you questions, which might change the conversation. And you'll notice that not everything I said made complete sense, like the part about 'meditative eyes,' as I don't even know what meditative eyes even means but I said it because I didn't know what else to say, and it doesn't have to make complete sense, because the way women think is very different than how men think. The point is that you're initiating a kind of conversation style that not every guy is doing. You're making statements, and pausing each time giving her a chance to respond. Each statement you make is essentially something that is trying to hook her, trying to get her to respond to either agree or disagree with you or to ask you a question.

In the case that she doesn't respond and you're running out of things to say, you have to make the decision based on her facial expressions as to whether you should continue to talk to her, or whether it's time for you to leave and find another woman who is more responsive. Also, notice with these statements that some of them are about her, and some of them are about you. This makes her feel good that you're giving thought and attention to her, and also gives her a bit of your own personality, and that's enough for her to decide if she wants to talk with you further or not.

If the woman verbally rejects you in any way, you simply say something like, "Ah, I understand, you're having a bad day, well it was nice meeting you," and then you simply smile and leave, because there's no point trying to push a conversation when your presence is not welcome.

If your statements get her to respond, and then the conversation goes quiet at some point, then you make more statements about something else to try to get the conversation going again. Also note, your statements need to be focused for the most part on a mix between her an you, possibly on the environment, but don't start talking about things that are obvious like the weather.

Also, another thing, if she says something negative to you, do not react to it, either ignore it or laugh at it like it's a joke. The reason being is that women will sometimes say negative things to see how you handle it. If you get upset, she'll see you as not a mentally strong man and your conversation with her will be over pretty quickly. For her to see you as a mentally strong man, you have to be non-reactive to any insult she throws your way. If she does tell you to go away though, you have to take that at face value and simply go away in a polite and non-reactive manner.

So you might be wondering, how can you tell if a negative comment from a woman is a rejection? Well, basically, if she makes fun of you in some way, it's not a rejection. For example, if she says, " You look like a clown" or "You seem weird." All that means is she wants to see if you're going to get all butt hurt or not. And in this case, turning it into a joke, such as saying "How did you know I was a clown? You must be a psychic. Yes, I am a clown, and I'm damn proud of it! I come from a long line of clowns. We help people, we make the world laugh," and then making a funny face would be an appropriate response, or just simply laughing at her comment would do, and ignoring the comment completely being unfazed by it and keeping things positive would also work. Remember, she's essentially testing what kind of man you are. However, if she says in an angry voice, "Get away from me!" or "I have a boyfriend," I'd consider that a rejection.

Also, don't ever make the mistake of making the conversation all about you and talking about yourself nonstop, as no one who doesn't know you wants to hear a lecture about how cool you are.

And another thing, don't try to impress the woman by talking about your amazing job, how much money you have, or your accomplishments or car, because most women will see that as a needy move, and needy moves will kill attraction. And any woman whose eyes light up when you start talking about how much money you have is not the kind of woman you want, because you don't want to get into a relationship with a woman who's just into you for your money, you don't need game for that, and since this is Poor Man's Game you should especially try to avoid those kinds of women.

If you have trouble coming up with statements on the spot, it's okay to write yourself an outline, and use the same outline on every woman you come across to get you through the first 20 to 40 minutes of conversation, and you can later modify your outline based on what has worked for you and what didn't work for you so that you'll do better the next time you approach a woman.

Look, most people don't realize it, but making statements, and keeping your body language in check, is very much key to building attraction with women. And if you're writing an outline, makes sure it's a little about you and a little about her. I get it, having a conversation making only statements seems hard if you're not used to it, but you'll get used to it. You could practice when you're in a room by yourself, looking at your outline and making statements to a wall, imagining you're talking to a woman, imagining how she'll respond, and how you should respond to her response.

Also, if a woman ignores you from the start but isn't telling you to go away, it means she's listening to your spiel, so just try to hang in there a tad bit longer than you think you should, because you never know, some women who play the silent game in the first few minutes may suddenly open up if you can hang in there just a little bit longer. But if you get any sense that she doesn't want you there, then of course bail, but do so politely, maybe ending with, "Well, I was trying hard to start a conversation with you, but you seem unresponsive so I'll go now, it was nice talking to you."

If you end it like that, she might suddenly realize that she enjoyed your company and say, "Hey, no, don't go, sorry, I was being so rude giving you the silent treatment. I didn't mean it, let's start again." If she says something like that, it's a really good sign. And believe it or not, that type of thing has happened to me many a time.

Everything I've just stated should help to get you through the first 20 to 40 minutes with a woman, and in a way where you're building attraction as opposed to simply asking a woman very basic job interview-type questions. But if you're at such a loss of what to say that you can't even get through 5 minutes of conversation or can't even get through the first 30 seconds, don't worry because I was like that at first. You'll get better and be able to talk longer naturally as you keep trying to communicate with women.

Every failure should make you feel frustrated and upset with yourself, which will make you think more seriously about how you could have made the interaction a better one, and that's exactly how you want to be thinking, because thinking like that will help you do better on each new approach. And doing better on each new approach will help you build the skill, the skill of talking to women. In fact, I'd say that if you're not making mistakes, and not trying to be better at the way in which you communicate with women, then you're doing something wrong, because making mistakes and learning from those mistakes is how we get better and improve at anything.

So it's fine if you make mistakes, as long as you are thinking about your mistakes, thinking about how you could have communicated in a better way, and taking that knowledge into future interactions with women. If you keep at it, and don't give up, you'll be a smooth-talking machine in no time at all. The point is to keep at it, not give up, and don't let those rejections get you down. Because the truth is each time you get rejected you learn something, and what you're learning is how to be a better man, and you're learning that from the best place that you could possibly be learning that, from real face-to-face contact with women.

CHAPTER 7
BUILDING CONNECTION

ONCE YOU'VE TALKED to the woman a bit (for 20 to 40 minutes), your next step is to get her to go somewhere else with you, either right now or at a later time.

To initiate this, you want to suggest that she go with you somewhere you were going to go anyway, this could be to a park, the supermarket, the laundromat, the library, to your apartment, or you name it, whatever you were going to do today, you tell her and you invite her along. You say something like, "I need to get to the library to take out a book, wanna come?" Or, "I need to go back home, because today's my cleaning day, wanna come?"

She's either going to say "Yes" or "No."

If she says "Yes," congrats, this is your first date.

If she says "No," she'll usually give a reason why, like maybe she has to pick up her little brother to take him somewhere or some other obligation. In that case, you should tell her something to the extent of, "I enjoyed talking with you and would like to hang out again," and ask for her number. Also, before you go, try to schedule with her. Don't call it a date, because the word 'Date' is a bit formal and implies a whole bunch of stuff, but that's what it is. Lastly, the day before the date, be sure to call or text her to confirm, unless you've scheduled for tomorrow, in which case no need to confirm.

Anyway, so either this woman decided to go somewhere directly with you after meeting her, or you've scheduled to meet with her and she showed up and you've got a date. Be aware that some women will flake, as in they will cancel or simply won't show, that will happen sometimes, don't sweat it, it's all part of the game. Should the woman ignore you or not show up, you simply send her a text or try to give her a call asking what happened, and see if she replies to your text or picks up the phone, and take it from there. Don't send more than one text or make more than one call. If you can't reach her, it's up to her to contact back or not.

So as for the date, you're basically not going to take her to any restaurant, because this is Poor Man's Game, rather you're going to take her to do something you normally do, as we've already established. And during that time, you want to get to know her better, because that's how you build connection. You essentially want her to do the majority of the talking, and you want to keep the conversation focused on her. It's fine at this point to ask her questions, but make sure they're questions about things she's talking about and not job interview-style questions. It's also fine to make jokes, but when she's talking you more or less want to listen to her and try to understand where she's coming from.

When you're listening to her, you want to validate her, this means when she's talking about something she likes, you can say something like, "Wow! That's so cool!" And when she's talking about something bad that happened to her, you can say something like, "That really sucks, I understand how you feel." Of course, if you have personal experiences with the same things you can bring those up, but don't go into too much detail about it, as she will learn about you later.

Because you are in the early stages of getting to know this

woman, you want to make sure that the conversation is almost never focused on you, the same as before, and pretty much only focused on her. Though it is good if during your date with her she at least knows just a little about you, as in what you regularly do for work or for fun, or something you like, but don't reveal too much or go into too much detail, because you have to give a woman something to wonder about when she's not with you. So keep most of the conversation focused on her.

Building a connection at this point in time means that you are basically a good listener who validates her feelings. However, you want to sprinkle in little samples of your personality and humor here and there.

Also, with whatever you're doing, whether it's checking a book out of the library or doing your laundry, it's fine to talk about the task at hand, and good if you can find ways where she can help, like ask her to drop the detergent in the washing machine while you move some other clothes into the dryer or something like that, this gets her more invested in you which will make her feel helpful. Be sure to thank her politely whenever she helps out with something and give her positive feedback where it may be appropriate.

After doing whatever you're doing with her, make sure you take her for a walk somewhere where you like to walk, and talk a little further with her, still keeping the conversation focused on her. This could be a busy main street, or it could be a park.

If you do everything right, the date will go just fine, and she'll have a good time even though she knows very little about you, and even though you haven't spent a dime on her.

CHAPTER 8
BEYOND THE FIRST DATE

OKAY, so you've been able to get through a first date and you've hopefully been able to establish some kind of connection with the woman, maybe it went well, or maybe it was a disaster, but however it went, your next step will be the same. Make sure you're in peak state and if you don't already have the woman's contact information, make sure you get that. You can just say, "Oh, by the way, I don't even know how to contact you," and pull out your phone, and she'll know what to do from there, or any other way you want to ask is fine.

Other than that, what you need to do next is go home. Tell her you really enjoyed her company, but you feel really beat and would like to go home, but also tell her as you look deeply into her eyes that you'd like to see her again and be sure to smile or wink when you say this indicating that something really amazing will happen next time, and then just go.

Go home and do whatever you normally do, and wait exactly 2 days before sending her a text. Also, during those 2 days, you need to meet a minimum of 2 more women, one on each day.

The woman you first met might text you before the 2 days pass, which is a good sign, but if not, you wait exactly 2 days and then you shoot her a text. In your text, you're going to say something like, 'Hey, I'd like to meet up tonight if you're free,' if she's not free and if she doesn't suggest another day and time, then you should suggest one more day and time, and if she's not free for that one, then you go silent and wait for her to suggest a day and time or say anything. If she doesn't text a day or time, then things will just be silent, it's on her to text you now or not, and you need to be okay with that. It's all fine, because you're meeting other women, at least one a day, right? So by the end of the week that will be 7 women you have met or more.

And anyway, if the woman is willing to come out, then it's in your best interest to get her to your place.

When you meet her, wherever you meet her, the conversation should be short, with you saying that you want to show her something whether you want to show her a book, have her meet your dog, or show her a really cool board game that you want to play with her. Whatever you tell her you want to show her, just make sure it's something plausible and fun sounding.

If she doesn't want to see what you want to show her and doesn't want to go along with you, then that's fine, and if that happens, you have to decide if you still want to hang out with her or if you want to leave. Usually, if on the second date a woman doesn't want to go to my place with me, I'll just make a sad face and leave, and that will be that. But that's up to you, if you really like this woman, then you can continue to run the date like you did the first date, and then if she comes out for a third date, then try to get her to your place once more.

If she's willing to go with you to see what you want to show her, then great! The second date is on!

At your place you show her what you said you would show her, let's say it's a book, and you tell her about the book in some detail for no more than 20 minutes, and then you switch things up and say something like, "Hey, I'd was wondering if we could talk about something."

She'll wonder what you want to talk about. And that's when you pause, look deep into her eyes, and then you want to say something like, "I really like you, but there's one question that I've been dying to know the answer to before we continue," and then you ask, "do you like soft kisses or hard kisses?"

And she's going to likely say one or the other.

And then you could answer, jokingly, "I'm not sure if I would feel comfortable doing that."

She is likely to either laugh or seem disappointed.

And then laugh, and say, "Just kidding."

Then you want to ask, "Not kidding this time, would you like me to kiss you right now?"

If she gives a dry or hesitant 'Yes,' then say something like, "I'm a man who believes in consent, you seem a bit hesitant, so I'm not going to kiss you unless I get an emphatic 'Yes' out of you."

And if you get that emphatic 'Yes,' then by all means kiss her.

And after the kiss, you want to ask more things, such as, "Would you like to make out?" And be sure to explain what that means if she doesn't know.

And if she gives an emphatic 'Yes' then don't disappoint her. However, be sure to check in with her during the make-out if she's doing okay and such, and be sure to ask for consent for any other things you want to do during the make-out that you didn't previously mention.

Everything mentioned above is just an example of how things could go, and it's entirely up to you if you want to ask her for a kiss or a hug, or whatever you're into.

The bottom line though, is that you want to ask for consent for every sexual act that you want to engage in with her, and you need that emphatic 'Yes' from her every time before proceeding, and she also needs to get an emphatic 'Yes' from you as well should she ask you to engage in any sexual acts. And if she doesn't ask you to engage in any sexual acts, then you might want to ask her, "Is there anything that you like that you want me to do?"

Also, if she ever goes silent, hesitates, or says 'No' when you ask her about doing something sexual, you need to let her know that it's okay if she doesn't want to do that with you, and that you could do something else or if she wants to leave that is also okay.

Hopefully though, she's at your place because she genuinely likes you, and you both have a wonderful, totally amazing, and memorable time together.

CHAPTER 9
AFTER SEX

SO YOU GOT LAID! Congrats! So now what? Well, that depends. You could tell her you have things to do, but you enjoyed your time together and you'd like to see her again and that you'll text her. Or if you really like her, and thinking maybe you'd like it if she became your girlfriend, you could invite her to spend the night. It's really up to you.

Since this is Poor Man's Game, if you invite her to spend the night, you need to confess to her that you're kind of broke and ask her if she could pitch in on tacos or spaghetti. If she offers to pay, that's great for you, but if not, well as we said you need to be self-sustainable so she needs to at least pitch in. If she likes you she'll pitch in. But if she's more broke than you, then you'll need to decide if you really want to be with a woman who's more broke than you, because if you do she'll make you poorer than you already are, so it's not the best idea if you're truly broke.

Yes, it's true what they say that 'money can't buy love,' but if you have love and you've only got one dollar to spare for a meal, then whoever wants to join you whether it's a woman, a friend, a family member, etc, had better pitch in or you risk going into negatives and starving. So if you do eat with the woman, you have to let her know your financial standing. And it's kind of best if she learns this after sex, since you'll both likely be hungry after sex, so if she hangs around she's going to find out.

Some might consider it rude to ask a woman to pitch in, but this is Poor Man's Game, and you shouldn't be ashamed of your financial status. If your financial status mattered to her she wouldn't have come on the second date, because on the first date it was pretty apparent that you didn't spend a single cent on the date, other than for your own stuff.

If a woman ever insists you pay or judges you, insisting that you have to pay for her, that's one that you probably have to let go, and not because you don't like her, but simply because you can't afford to have a woman like that in your life. It's true though, there are women out there who do not want to be in a relationship with a poor man, but there are a lot more women out there who are perfectly fine to be in a relationship with a poor man, and those are the ones you're going for, all others you, unfortunately, have to let go.

CHAPTER 10
TO GIRLFRIEND OR NOT TO GIRLFRIEND

IF YOU'RE THINKING about stopping your process of meeting new women, and you want to settle on a girlfriend, it means you're out of the game at that point. And that's fine if you want to go that route, there's nothing wrong with it.

However, before you make the decision to keep a woman as your girlfriend because you genuinely like her, all you really need is that she accept you for who you are, unrelated to your financial status, and that she is genuinely into you, and that she brings happiness to your life and doesn't have any behaviors that would add stress to your life. Any woman that meets all of those criteria is going to pretty likely be a keeper.

But you also need to realize that if you decide to make one woman your girlfriend, then you're giving up quite a bit, as in you're giving up all the other women you've already met, and all the women that you will meet in the future. So is it really worth it to you to give all that up for just one woman? You need to think about that very seriously. That one woman had really better be something extra special for you to give up your whole Poor Man's Game lifestyle, because it's really an awesome lifestyle.

It can be difficult when you really like a woman and she really likes you back to have to give up your lifestyle, but if you're sick of your lifestyle or if you only got into this life-style in the first place because deep down you simply wanted a girlfriend by your side, then it makes sense to settle down, go the girlfriend route, and perhaps even eventually get married.

But if you're like me, then you might choose to never settle down, and to keep on meeting new women all the time, and to have several regulars who meet you on different days of the week. Once you have that set up going, it's really hard to give that up for any one woman. The choice is yours though, and I'll always respect your decision no matter which way you go.

CHAPTER 11
MANAGING MANY WOMEN

IF YOU KEEP at Poor Man's Game, and you keep meeting new women every day, and some months or years pass. It's going to be harder and harder to be able to schedule every woman, and you're going to find yourself having to drop some in favor of others that you like more. And eventually, you'll find some really special women who will be okay with not being your girlfriend, but seeing you regularly and even being kind enough to buy you a meal when they spend time with you. I have 4 women like that in my life, one is my Monday woman, one is my Tuesday woman, one is my Wednesday woman, and one is my Thursday woman. These women are my regulars, and have been loyal to me for a very long time, and so I'm likewise loyal to them, or as loyal as a man in an open relationship can be. And you'll eventually have regulars too if you do things exactly the way I do them.

And Friday through Sunday is all about meeting new women for me. Yes, I still keep approaching just one woman a day, and I don't have time to schedule them all. I have so many women's contact details that I don't even need to meet one woman a day anymore per se, but I still choose to do so, solely for the purpose of keeping my game skills sharp.

Anyway, before you get to the point where I'm at, you'll eventually over time accumulate the contact details of many different women in your phone, some you'll have met for a second date and some you won't have met for a second date and the situation with each one will be different. It's good if you can write notes in each one's profile in whatever contact app you have on your phone to jog your memory of what happened when you met them. Because when you have a day where no date is set up, you'll want to shoot out a text to multiple women in your phone at once and see who bites and wants to meet up with you. If more than one bites, you'll have to choose which one you're going to meet today, and which one you're going to have to text something like "Ah, apologies, something came up and I can't meet today anymore, how about next week on Friday?"

Also important, is that you get really good with whatever calendar app you have in your phone, because you really want to not make scheduling mistakes, because things can quickly become a mess when you know hundreds or thousands of women and don't fully understand your calendar app.

CHAPTER 12
ENJOY THE JOURNEY

WE'RE COMING to the end of this book, and I'd like to make it clear that Poor Man's Game is more than just some method, it is a journey that occurs over a long period of time of meeting and talking with many different women until you find the ones who are open to the idea of being with a man who is not financially successful, but possesses a great degree of financial intelligence; you know, things like how to save a buck or two by eating at home, and the importance of getting things a bit cheaper at the supermarket by being aware of discounts and using coupons. Women you meet don't have to care about discounts, coupons, and bargain hunting, but they need to respect that you care about it. And likewise, they need to respect that they'll always have to pay their half of the bill, even when it comes to home-cooked meals.

Yes, there are many men who will just pay for whatever for a woman, but in a way that's a form of sexism. If men and women are truly equal, then it makes sense that each would pay their half as far as anything they eat or anything they do together.

Now when you start this journey, you'll be tempted to buy a coffee for a woman at a cafe or to take her out for a burger, but I say, "Don't do it!" Because once you set that frame, the woman will always expect you to be the one paying. Maybe you make a decent wage, but if you're going to be meeting thousands upon thousands of women over many years, the cost to you for buying all those coffees and meals adds up to quite a significant chunk of change. So I highly urge you to not go that route. You need to not be afraid of the fact that the woman might walk away. In fact, every woman that walks away is a good thing, because that's one less woman that you know is not a good fit for you. You see, you need to have a filtering process with these women, and women okay with the fact that it's important to you to spend as little as possible on anything is exactly the kind of woman that you want to be with.

So you see it's going to be a journey for you, a journey of meeting many kinds of different women, and you'll need to get some of these many different kinds of women to go somewhere else with you so you can build a connection with them, and you'll hopefully have an amazing time with all the women who choose to go with you. And either you'll end up with a girlfriend out of it, or you'll end up with many regulars like me and still going out there and meeting new women when you have time.

It's not an easy journey and you should expect a lot of rejection. But if you keep at it, if you keep meeting new women, you'll soon find yourself to be one of the happiest men alive, because you'll realize that you have so many options with women that you don't know what to do with or how to schedule them all.

So whether you really are poor, or whether you're actually not poor at all but tired of spending money on women, money that could be better used for other purposes, you'll greatly benefit for implementing everything you've learned in this book into your life, because it will be a great life for you, and all on your terms. A lot of guys have women and money troubles, but you won't have women troubles at all, perhaps money troubles, but definitely not women troubles, at least not if you're following what I've stated to do in this book.

Anyway, I wish you the best of success on your journey, and hope you find and meet many wonderful women who can help add great amounts of joy and happiness to your life.

NEWSLETTER

Oh, hello again. I would just like to inform you that my publisher, Soy Sauce Publishing, runs a secret newsletter called Real Game, where you can get notifications about new books similar to this one, as well as various discounts and special offers.

To join Real Game, all you need to do is go to the following URL:

SoySaucePublishing.com/RealGame

Also, I may sometimes write you something through that newsletter, so it's a way of hearing more from me, so really hope you subscribe.

ACKNOWLEDGEMENTS

I'd like to thank my dad, Eliezer Holser, of whom I never would have learned to approach women without. And I'd like to thank my mother, Blossom Holser, who gave me life, bringing me into this wonderful world.

I'd also like to thank my good friend, Oliver Rockhurst, for giving me a lot of support and advice when I first said I was going to write this book.

And I'd also like to thank all of my friends out there who supported me throughout the many years of my life, even though none of them wanted to be named in this book due to the subject matter, but I don't blame them.

And lastly, I'd like to thank you, my dear reader, for being so kind as to purchase this book and help support the spread of Poor Man's Game. Thank you so much.